# The Little Ideas Notebook

Copyright © 2020 by Belinda McLean

Print ISBN: 978-0-6450554-0-5

1st Edition

www.belindamclean.com

# How to use

Your ideas are valuable. So many amazing ideas are lost when they aren't written down or mapped out.

This book is for those ideas.

There's lined & blank pages so you can write down your thoughts as well as draw diagrams, doodle or do whatever comes creatively to you on the blank pages.

Write them down.

Draw them out.

Enjoy the process... and then the REAL fun starts; putting them into ACTION!

*Belinda McLean*

www.ingramcontent.com/pod-product-compliance
Lightning Source LLC
Chambersburg PA
CBHW050303010526
44108CB00040B/2244